PARLOR
GAMES

PARLOR
GAMES

A BULFINCH PRESS BOOK
Little, Brown and Company
Boston · Toronto · London

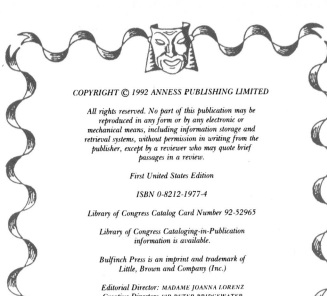

First United States Edition

ISBN 0-8212-1977-4

Library of Congress Catalog Card Number 92-52965

*Library of Congress Cataloging-in-Publication
information is available.*

*Bulfinch Press is an imprint and trademark of
Little, Brown and Company (Inc.)*

Editorial Director: MADAME JOANNA LORENZ
Creative Director: SIR PETER BRIDGEWATER
Text: PAUL BARNETT ESQUIRE
Original Illustrations: COLONEL IVAN HISSEY

The Publishers would like to thank all those who kindly
gave permission to use visual materials in this book.

PRINTED IN HONG KONG

CONTENTS

CONCERNING *the* GREED *for* GLORY

LIFE ITSELF IS BUT A GAME; *albeit a game whose* GREAT ARBITER *controls the pattern of the play: what a cruel game it would be, without the Guiding Benevolence of He Who observes us as we partake in our daily round! Yet there are lesser games, in which we may indulge, to use our leisure time in the pursuit of goals less momentous. Too often such games, in these* **corrupting times**, *are rowdy and near-blasphemous (I refer, of course, to the indulgence in such crass sports as cricket on the Lord's Own Day); worse still, their participants desire above all else the glory of triumph, rather than the greater joy of taking part.* SUCH GREED FOR GLORY WILL DESTROY MEN'S SOULS!

The games herein, if practised by the pure of heart, are innocent, wholesome and may even serve to improve. Yet the reader must be warned that even these may be perverted by the **FOE OF OUR SOULS** *to become lures for self-aggrandisement. I thus beg of you to recall, in Master Herrick's words, that:*

In prayer the lips ne'er act the winning part,
Without the sweet concurrence of the heart!

ARMYTAGE WARE, M.A. (OXON), D.D.
(ST. ANDREWS), 31ST DECEMBER, 1899

THE BEST BEVERAGE FOR CHILDREN

CADBURY'S COCOA is closely allied to milk in the large proportion of flesh-forming & strength-sustaining elements that it contains. It is prepared on the principle of excluding the superabundance of fatty indigestible matter with which cocoa abounds —supplying a refined thin infusion of absolutely pure cocoa, exhilarating and refreshing, for Breakfast, Luncheon, Tea, or Supper —giving staying power, and imparting new life and vigour to growing Children, and those of delicate constitutions.

CADBURY'S COCOA | ABSOLUTELY PURE, THEREFORE BEST.

PREFACE *to* 1924 EDITION

My esteemed Great Uncle, *Dr. Armytage Ware,* love him dearly though I might, was a crusty and cantankerous old devil at the best of times, with about as much sense of humour as a whalebone corset. His chief sources of amusement, as I recall, were dressing up his furniture in elaborately hand-embroidered garments and writing comic songs in Sanskrit (*"And, Lo! The distinguished Emperor of the Numibians has trodden on his hem and fallen"* is a classic of its type, and caused a riot at family Christmases).

Still, to give the old boy his due, his book of INDOOR PARTY GAMES, although infamous in the livelier circles I move in, has sold and sold, with the result that the canny Grandson ("Spiffy" Harbottle – you may know 🖝

him, we were at school together actually) of Ware's original publisher has asked me, the last of the Ware clan, to edit a new edition (something about *"preserving the memory of your revered ancestor"* – which is Spiffy slang for *"let's cash in while the going's good, with all royalties to a needy cause"*).

Anyway, the really good news is that I have managed to slip in amongst Armytage's worthy but brain-stressing *Victorian delights* more than a few racy stinkers for the flappers and jocks of the *jazz age*. (And let me tell you, the lost generation knew precisely where it was until we arrived on the scene!!) These were devised by myself and my pal "Buffy" Bryson over a series of hilarous weekends at Spiffy's country pile. They're not exactly intellectual (as you might expect from a chap who was – harshly, I would contend – sent down from Eton at fourteen for putting blancmange in his Housemaster's underwear, thus missing out on the finer points of education), but for like-minded types my "contact sports for the drawing-room classes" will stimulate the fun-glands like chilled Bubbly. **FEEDING THE ZOO** is my personal favourite – it catches me out every time I play. Here goes, and good gaming!!

FREDDIE DUFF-WARE, 1924

CHARADES

Here is a game that may be played with great propriety, by both young and old in the family; yet has its perils, for, as Mr. Thackeray disapprovingly growled, it encourages *"the many ladies among us who have beauty to display their charms, and the fewer number who have cleverness to exhibit their wit."* But, if seemly played, it provides many an opportunity for harmless drollery.

Two of the company are elected to absent themselves from the room, where the rest may while away the time with light conversation. **Scheming with mischief**, the brace of conspirators beyond the door must decide upon a word that the remainder of the company can then guess from their enactment of its syllables.

Let us say that our conspirators have selected SACRAMENTAL as their word. This may deem to be analysed as *SACK*, and *RAM*, and *MENTAL*. It is now their task to devise three playlets, which they may perform singly or between themselves, in such a wise that their audience may guess each syllable and then – a fourth playlet – the word all told. Thus: a Santa Claus is laden with a *Sack;* a farmer dodges and cavorts as he seeks to avoid the attentions of a stamping and enmaddened *Ram!;* a Gypsy uses her sham *Mental* powers to detect the fortunes of a naïve customer who has *"crossed her palm with silver"*; all this to be done in silence. (Some play the game with speech, but thereby they destroy their pleasure.) Then, at last, our players may ☞

with all solemnity, portray the grave mystery of the blessed.

As each playlet is enacted, the audience shall call out their impressions of the syllable that is the subject. Thus, for the first, *"COALMAN!"* they may cry; or *"TWEENIE!"*; until such time as one among them infers correctly. At such point the performers shall desist their play, and indicate with a nod the correctness of that supposition; whereon they proceed to the next of their scenes.

Much improvement of the mind may be enjoyed thereby by the youngest of the family, who are thus introduced to words with which earlier they had been unfamiliar. For those wiser, there is the opportunity for much decorous mirth.

THE GAME

Perhaps I should rather have headed this Chapter **THE QUEEN'S GAME**, for it is widely reported that this above all is the game Our Gracious Majesty enjoys playing the most when the company around her is relaxed. It is a pleasure which HER LOYAL SUBJECTS may appreciate sharing with their Monarch.

The company divides into two teams of equal number and constitution, so that the elder are mixed judiciously with the youngest. Each team must then write down on a sheet of paper a predetermined number of literary or theatrical titles, or perhaps of contemplative proverbs,

*which they are desirous of setting their oppo-
nents to unmask. (Or it may be, if there is an
odd-man-out, that he singly devises such a list-
ing for the challenging of both teams.)*

*A person from the first team approaches those
of the second, and it is covertly imparted to him
what his task must be. He then returns to his
own team and silently proceeds to mime for their
benefit the phrase in question. Should it be the
TITLE OF A BOOK, he first indicates with
open palms that this is so; for a PLAY he mimes
the opening of curtains; for a PROVERB, he
may place his fist against his forehead, demon-
strating appropriate profundity of thought.
Then, by raising his fingers, he tells his fellows
how many words there are in the phrase he
wishes cryptically to divulge to them.*

This information communicated, the actor raises a single finger to show that he is about to commence miming the first word. This he may do in a single fit, or **syllable-by-syllable**. *There may be pre-arranged indications for common words, like "And", and "A", and "The" – it is not infrequent, for instance, that "The" be registered by placing the forefinger of one hand horizontally over the vertically raised forefinger of the other. And, should a word or a part of a word prove beyond his thespian abilities to mime, he may instead enact a word of similar sound, perhaps a word that rhymes; that he is engaging in such an exercise he indicates by cupping a hand to his ear, or pulling on it gently.*

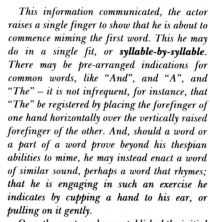

Once the company have established the initial word, the performer then proceeds to the second, and so the game continues. Once all has been guessed, it is the turn of the opposing company to be quizzed in like manner. And so it continues until it is time for tea.

WHISTLING BISCUITS

*D*ivide the party into two equal teams: if there is an odd number, the person left over will be umpire. The teams stand in line abreast facing each other, and every player has two cream crackers, or water biscuits. On a given signal, the first player in each team may start to *eat their crackers*: as soon as their mouth is clear enough to whistle, the second player in the team can start to eat and so on. The first team in which all the players have whistled wins the contest.

PROVERBS

"Nothing ever becomes real till it is experienced – even a proverb is no proverb to you till your life has illustrated it." How true are the words of Master Keats. The saws that we exchange among ourselves, day in and day out, morning, noon and perhaps night also, may serve to **improve our minds** and maintain our morality; yet words are one thing and experience another; until we have enacted the *MEANING* of those sayings we may not fully grasp their import, or comprehend their significance entirely. It is among the **Great Pleasures** (and there are many others) of this pastime that those who participate therein may gain fresh insight into old saws, and thereby, if eager learners, enhance their own virtues.

One of the company leaves the room. In his absence, the remainder decide among themselves a suitably inspirational 🐾

proverb that shall be their subject; say the absent one is of gloomy disposition, they may select some apposite epigram like the *Venerable Tusser*'s remark that, *"Till you can sing and rejoice and delight in God, as misers do in gold, and kings in sceptres, you never enjoy the world"*; or perhaps some other fittingly succinct distillation of wisdom.

On the return of *Master Singleton*, their glum comrade, he must ask of each of them a question in turn; their responses must contain the words of the proverb in order. Thus, should he inquire of the first: "What is your name?"; the reply should be, mayhap: "Must you wait *till* we have been wed these twenty years ere you discover my name?"; or some other such fresh - faced jollity. Of the second he demands: "Where do you live?"; and is informed: "Near to the Church where *you* worship of a Sunday"; and so the questioning and answering proceed until, after perhaps four or five such exchanges, the full expression of the proverb is evident to the guesser, and all is gaiety. Then another must take his turn.

SOME VERSATILE PROVERBS
THAT YOU MIGHT USE

— ◆ —

- *Wilful Waste Makes Woeful Want*
- *Lucky at Cards, Unlucky in Love*
- *Gaming, Women and Wine; While They Laugh, They Make Men Pine*
- *Beauty's Sister is Vanity, and her Daughter Lust*
- *Only a Bad Workman Disputes with His Tools*
- *There's No Fool Like an Old Fool*
- *Hell Hath No Fury Like a Woman Scorned*
- *When the Wine is In the Wit is Out*
- *Fair Face, Foul Heart*
- *A Little Rain Layeth Much Dust*

ADVERBS

*H*ere is another guessing game in which one of the party must needs first leave the room, while the others scheme. *Their pleasurable task* it is to determine upon an adverb, which might be JOYOUSLY; or MIRTHFULLY; or MOROSELY; or DEMURELY. (The *paterfamilias* may require to curb the **frivolous instincts** of the youthful, as otherwise they may select coarse and risible adverbs such as LICENTIOUSLY; or INDECOROUSLY; or some other such lewdness.) On the return of Master Singleton to the room, his companions must disport themselves in accordance with the selected adverb. He may request of one of them to perform some chore, such as giving air to a nursery song; should the chosen adverb be MOURNFULLY, then the individual must do so with a long face and many a squeezed tear; the remainder meanwhile chorus their sobs. And so forth. The truth guessed, the next person must depart for *temporary solitude*.

SPIN *the* TRENCHER

*Children in especial love this simple, vigorous diversion. What are required are a round trencher, platter or plate, wooden for preference, and either a bread-board on the floor or a table set in the centre of a clear space; around this the players seat themselves in **a voluptuous circle**; they should not be permitted to have drinks or sweetmeats, as else these may be spilled. The first player places the trencher upright on the bread-board, and gives it a spin; as so doing, he calls out the name of another of the company, and retreats post-haste. It is the part of the other to reach the trencher in good time to catch it afore it falls; if he fails, he is counted out of the game; should he succeed, he lives to play another time. Either way, his next task is to **spin the trencher**, like the other preceding him; and call out a name; and so the game continues until only one is left; or all become fractious.*

CRAMBO

THIS IS A guessing game of ancient origin, and the meaning of its name has been lost in the mists of antiquity; although some lexicographers speculate its derivation from the Latin phrase *"Crambe Repetita"*; meaning "cabbage served up again". It seems the game itself sprang from a simple rhyming game, also once called CRAMBO, whereby a first person utters the first line of an imaginary poem; then his companion produces a second line, with due observation to metre and rhyme, but containing not one word repeated from the first. But that is a dry and tiresome pastime; unlike the game here portrayed!

Once more the *paterfamilias* summons one of the company and bids him leave the room, and the remainder select a word among themselves. We shall imagine this word to be *FICKLE*; for it is not unseemly to use such occasions to gently advert to the foibles of our fellows, thereby hopefully exercising a tacit influence for improvement upon their characters. On the return of Master Singleton they give him a word as a clue to the one he seeks; this is not the word itself, but one rhyming with it, usually of very different meaning; so

that they might say: *"PICKLE"*. He must then attempt to deduce the word, and ask of them questions seeking to elicit an

affirmative response. Yet he must not interrogate them directly as to his speculations; rather his inquiries must allude by definition. Thus, he may say: "Is it a sharp blade, used by the tiller of soil in harvesting his crops?"; to which they will respond, **"No, it is not a sickle!"** Or he might ask: *"Is it a dark rye bread, of coarse texture, as is to be expected of its Westphalian origin?"*; and, once they have recovered their composure in the wake of this sally, they will return: **"No, it is not pumpernickel"**. Master Singleton may suffer a forfeit should all his investigations come to naught; yet also the other members of the company may forfeit, should they in their turn be unable to establish the words which he has insinuated.

CRAMBO II:
DUMB CRAMBO

This game is more energetic than the previous more august form, and thus perhaps holds greater attraction for the *younger and more exuberant members* of the company; while, perhaps, their more mature counterparts pass their time elsewhere in discussion of weightier issues.

The Laws of the game are as before; but now Master Singleton may not *inquire* pertaining to his guesses but must instead *enact* them. (For reasons patent, all the subject-words need be verbs.) Thus, if the clue he has been given upon his return be the word *"SKIP"*, he must mime *Sip*ping; or *Trip*ping; or *Nip*ping; or Bull*whip*ping; or *Equip*ping; or some such like. Nor must the company speak in their responses; rather they must *hiss* their disapproval, until Master Singleton triumphs by his parade of Wor*ship*ping!

Forfeits may be paid by the company should they be adjudged to have failed to guess correctly a word well-mimed by the actor. It is as wise for an older member of the party to be present as arbiter.

BUZZ

· 7 · 7 · 7 · 7 ·

If you happen to have among the company an expert mathematician, it is unwise to play ***BUZZ***: but even he may be taken off his guard, for the essence of Buzz is speed. It consists simply of counting: the first player says "One", the second "Two", and so on. But the player whose turn it

would be to say "Seven" must, instead of that number, say "Buzz"; and likewise "Buzz" must take the place of every number which contains SEVEN or *ANY MULTIPLE* of SEVEN: that is 7, 14, 17, 21, 27, 28, 35, 37, 42, 47, and so on for all the rest.

Probably most of the players will have dropped out before you reach 69 and the long succession of buzzes that follows it! Do try it. *It's maddening!*

SHADOW PICTURES

Even the poorest of draftsmen can catch the likenesses of his friends with telling verisimilitude.

Take a sheet of paper, white on one side and black on the other, and pin it to the wall so that the white side faces the room. Next place a bright light on a table at an appropriate distance from the wall, and ask the person whose portrait is about to be drawn to step between the light and the wall and to stand perfectly still. Because our subject will cast a sharp silhouette on the paper, anyone can easily move a pencil around the outline of the shadow.

Remove the paper from the wall, go over the lines again where they may not be clear, and cut out the drawing. Now all one has to do is to reverse the cut-out, stick it onto a white piece of paper, and the result is a black silhouette.

GHOSTS

Here is a game that is best played on the *Eve of All Hallowmas*, when, so Godless tradition has it, the spirits of the Dead are at Large across the Land. Such Pagan belief, vile in itself, may yet give rise to pleasing enough diversions for the young, so long as it is explained to them sombrely beforehand that such matters are ONLY DREAMS AND PHANTASIES, like fairies (although my friend, the Rev. Mar. Gentle, of Cottingley Parsonage, has imparted to me *disturbing tales* in this context; the which I shall not bore you with now). With the lights turned up bright, to banish spooks!, adults and children alike may divert themselves with this harmless and educational game.

There may be any number of players, all accoutred at the outset with four "*LIVES*"; the first of the party must supply an initial letter. The second follows this up with a next letter; and then the third, a third. These three letters must all run together, in order, so that they may be the start of a word; thus "C", "O", "N", will be a valid beginning, while "R", "Q", "Z", or other such foolishness, will not. (It would be better the frivolous were instead adjured to douse their over-excitability in perusal of some improving text until such time as they were more meetly prepared to enjoy themselves.)

Now the others must, in turn, contribute each the next letter, all the while bearing in mind that the letter they supply must still render the whole a legitimate beginning to a real word; also that they must not themselves supply a letter such that a word be concluded.

EXAMPLE: Imagine that the players so far have announced "C", "O", "N", "C", "E", and "P"; the next of their number envisages that the entire word might be "CONCEPTION", and so Master Simpleton says "T". But then how his fellows *mirthfully* deride him! for has he not inadvertently completed a word, albeit not the

34

word he had had in mind! And clever, too, his predecessor in the round, for Master Simpleton had no option but to complete this word. Yet he might have said: "R". Then would the company have been mystified, for might it not be that there is a word commencing: "CONCEPR"? The next player in turn might choose to believe there was, in which case he could add another letter; but, wiser, he might instead challenge Master Simpleton to explain himself; upon which Master Simpleton will break down and confess tearfully that indeed he knows of no word starting in this wise; whereupon he loses one of his *"lives"*, and becomes a *"one-quarter ghost"*. But, should he be able to recite a word appropriate to the occasion, then it is the challenger who must don the cap of Master Simpleton and lose a *"life"*. In either event, that is the conclusion of that fit of the game; and it must renew with Master Simpleton providing an initial letter. Matters proceed thus until all but one player have lost four *"lives"*, to become *"ghosts"*; whereupon that person is declared **THE VICTOR.**

GHOSTS II: STRONG SPIRITS

*T*he name of this game is not reference to the Demon, but instead to the fortitude of those who would participate; for if GHOSTS itself is a test of the nerve and intellect, STRONG SPIRITS! can cause even the most extensively learned to fret the succeeding night away, in consideration of letters they *might* have proffered, if only . . . Indeed, the game is of such difficulty, and the time between players' essays consequently so *protracted*, that often it is wise to use paper and pencil to record the turns, and to have books to hand for perusal as others *wrestle with their wits!*

The rules are as before; excepting that players may add letters not just *after* those that have earlier been contributed, but also *in front of them*. Thus, if to date the letters are "C", "O", and "N", as before, a next player may append, *exempli gratia*, an "S" or "E", ahead of those, with words in mind being perhaps "S*cone*", or "S*conce*", or "S*econd*", or even "R*econciliation*"!

This game may last some little while . . .

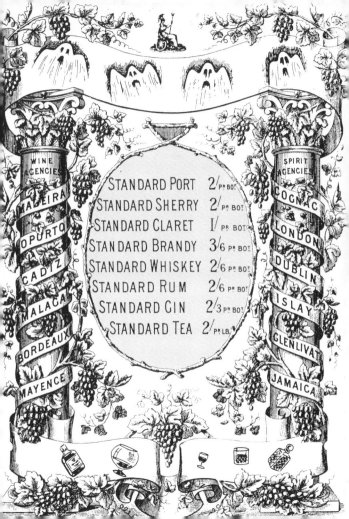

STANDARD PORT 2/ PR BOT
STANDARD SHERRY 2/ PR BOT
STANDARD CLARET 1/ PR BOT
STANDARD BRANDY 3/6 PR BOT
STANDARD WHISKEY 2/6 PR BOT
STANDARD RUM 2/6 PR BOT
STANDARD GIN 2/3 PR BOT
STANDARD TEA 2/ PR LB.

WINE AGENCIES
MADEIRA
OPORTO
CADIZ
MALAGA
BORDEAUX
MAYENCE

SPIRIT AGENCIES
COGNAC
LONDON
DUBLIN
ISLAY
GLENLIVAT
JAMAICA

MOUSEHOLE

Some call this game MIDDLEDITCH; *others*
MELTON MOWBRAY; *when played using the
titles of the streets of the English Metropolis
rather than the place-names of the Country, it
is often termed* MORNINGTON CRESCENT.
*But here we honour one rather more charming
resort, where oftentimes it has been the pleasure
of myself and my family to spend a week in quiet
contemplation, breathing fresh, invigorating
ozone, far from Slough and its grimy cares.*

  *It is the duty of the first player to enunciate
the name of a town or hamlet somewhere in
England (the more adventurous gamesters may*

enlarge their scope to include American Colonial or Antipodean locations); the task of the next player is then to speak the name of another, whose first letter must be identical with the concluding letter of the previously-given name. Let us say that the starter of the game had said: "SLOUGH" (though it is hard to imagine why); it is the obligation of the next to respond with "HARLESDEN", or "HESSAFORD", or perhaps even Essex's "HELION'S BUMPSTEAD"; but NOT with "HEXHAM", or any other name that ends with the letter "M", for that would permit the succeeding contestant to contribute, in triumph, the name: "MOUSEHOLE!"

Cunning and foresightful players may elect to use this game to educate their fellows, especially the children, who will naturally be athirst for enlightenment, by choosing names whose spellings are oft ill-rendered, viz: "ASHBY DE LA ZOUCH" (to which the unwary may affix an "E"), "BABBACOMBE" (from which the ignorant may omit the final "E"), and others too many to muster. Thus the slow-witted may derive benefit, and the remainder, merriment.

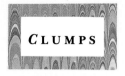

CLUMPS

As we all know, a *"Clump"*, is a "thick, short, shapeless piece of anything", or so Messrs. Chambers' dictionary informs us; but that tells us little or nothing of this venerable game; as neither do its other soubriquets, *"Clubs"*, and *"Chumps"*.

One of the company is elected to start the game, and to serve as MASTER OF THE QUESTIONS until it is another's turn. He must silently determine an object; it is the task of the remainder of the party to infer the precise nature of that object, deriving their clues solely through interrogating the MASTER OF QUESTIONS, who may respond to their questions only monosyllabically, with either a "Yes", or a "No". All told, no more than twenty questions may be asked and answered; should the inquisitors fail in their pleasurable chore, then the MASTER OF THE QUESTIONS is deemed the winner, and he must select another item as his *secret;* but in the event that one of the company succeeds in identifying the object before the twenty questions are up, then the role of MASTER OF THE QUESTIONS is passed to him; and so it continues. ━

But the contestants do not enter the fray unarmed! No: at the very outset the MASTER OF THE QUESTIONS must supply them with an hint – advice as to whether the object be "*Animal*", or "*Vegetable*", or "*Mineral*", or perhaps a mixture of two or more of these. By "*Animal*", is meant, not only living creatures (fish and insects among them), but also things that have been derived therefrom; to wit meat, or leather, or woollen or silken clothing, or any number of other items found about the home. By "*Vegetable*", likewise, is indicated all the contents of the Plant Kingdom that Carolus Linnaeus himself might desire, and also articles that trace their origins to such: paper and wood and cotton are exemplars. Fin-

ally, by "*Mineral*", we refer to any thing that is or is made from neither plant nor animal (although Water and Air are generally not reckoned, being too pervasive).

Imagine, then, that our MASTER OF THE QUESTIONS has opted for **"A CHRISTMAS DINNER"**. He must immediately announce to all that this is "*Animal, Vegetable, and Mineral*"; for the goose is (or, until its demise, was) an animal, albeit a rather

ill-tempered one, and hence deserving of
extinction (although we must not be too
hasty with our harshness, for perhaps it was
a very descendant of one of those that saved
Rome with their clacking!); the vegetables
are of necessity of vegetable origin (despite
the travails of the cook); and the seasonings
will inevitably (excepting oversight) contain salt, which is a
mineral. The company may then (except in the most over-
pious of households) ask: "Is the animal a human?" To
which the MASTER OF THE QUESTIONS will respond:
"No." "Is it dead?" one of them might carol intelligently.
"Yes," will come the reply. "Can you wear it?" might be
the succeeding inquiry . . . And so the interrogation will
proceed.

A different way to play is for each person in turn to
be the MASTER OF THE QUESTIONS. There is, in this
variant, no limit to the number of inquiries that
may be made, and the game continues until at last
the matter is solved. The number of questions required
is recorded; and, when all is done, he whose conundrum
required the most questioning is declared THE LAUREATE.

CLUMPS II:
BOTTICELLI

*I*t was with a heavy heart that I wrote the name at the top of this page; but I am obliged by tradition to leave it thus. It is no responsibility of mine that the game is not rather titled something a little more robust and yeomanishly stolid, like *STUBBS*, or *TURNER*. Certainly *LANDSEER* would have been preferable, the favour of Our Adored Monarch outweighing any suspicion we might have about his appellation. However, we are stuck with this name; and must make the best of it.

The rules of this otherwise perfectly enjoyable game are the same as those for *Clumps;* but here the MASTER OF THE QUESTIONS selects instead a notable historical personage (preferably not some obscure foreign daubster), and adopts that person's character as his own. Again twenty questions are permitted; and answers must be "Yea," or "Nay," as for example: *"Are you still living?"* – "Yes"; *"Are you female?"* – "No"; *"Are you an obscure foreign daubster?"* – "No!"

STOUTSTOMACH HOTEL,
B. G. PAUNCH, Proprietor.
GOOD LIVING: SWEET BEDS:
LIBERAL CHARGES.
TURKEYVILLE,
W.T.

THE TRAVELLER'S ALPHABET

ere is a test of one's Vocabulary and Syntax, not to mention one's Geography! All may derive not only entertainment but also that delight which gave Francis Bacon to remark: "*All knowledge and wonder* (which is the seed of knowledge) is an impression of pleasure in itself."

It is the role of the first player to select the name of a place that begins with the letter "A"; and thus to say: "I am going to Andover" (or whichever might be the locale he has opted for). The player to his left must inquire: "*And what shall you do in Andover?*", to which the first replies with a sentence in which all four of the *verb*, *adverb*, *noun* and *adjective* must begin with that same initial letter; *exempli gratia*: "I shall artfully avoid

ambiguous anagrams." This success recorded, it is now the turn of the player to the left to say: "I am going to Bognor Regis" (as well he might indeed be; but failing that, to "Birmingham", or "Billericay", or some other such); and, on receiving the germane query, he might retort: "I shall belligerently bully Basildonian bulldogs."

So the game advances. Should "Q" be successfully negotiated, which is by no means easy; and then some-one found a plausible reason for venturing to Slough; sooner or later the wits of all will be challenged by "X", and "Z". For "X", one must foray beyond our shores – perhaps to Xuzhou, which is frequented by such Chinees as find the attractions of the place irresistible; but, turning to "Z", in England one may choose to go to Zeal Monachorum, in Devonshire, Zeals or Zeals Knoll, in Wiltshire, or Zelah, Zennor or Zennor Head, in Cornwall; less fastidiously, one might venture to Zoar, but that is in Scotland.

OBSTACLE RACE

Choose two from the party and send them
out of the room. The rest then rearrange
the furniture and ornaments to form an
obstacle course up and down its length.
The two are then brought back and
told that their task is to run a blindfold obstacle course up the room and
back, and that the winner will be given a
prize. They are given half a minute to memorize
the position of the barriers before being blindfolded and moved to the starting line. While
this is happening the other members of the party
silently remove all of the objects, so the route is
perfectly clear. It is very amusing to all to then
watch the two in their race, step-
ping high and making futile little
leaps around the room.

An alternative is to set the
course using eggs, and to explain to the "RUNNERS" that the
carpet is new or unwashable.

While the blindfolds are being
tied, the eggs are picked up, and
cream crackers or water biscuits scattered all across the
floor. With every step the
runners will think they have
broken an egg, and in their
panic they will dance higher
and higher.

MURDER

Everyone is given a folded piece of paper — these are all blank except one that says "DETECTIVE" *and one that says* "MURDERER". *Whoever gets these named cards will adopt these roles, but must not reveal their identity.* The host or hostess then announces that everyone must be on their guard: the police have phoned earlier to say they have a tip-off that a murder is to be committed. The murderer is already in their midst, and will kill silently. The victim will receive a pat on the back, but death is certain, and they will have no choice but to scream and fall. However, if it is any consolation, a famous detective is present, and the death will be swiftly avenged. The DETECTIVE then announces his or her identity, and leaves the room.

Then the lights are turned off. Considerable movement follows, with players stealing softly to wherever in the room they believe that safety lies. The MURDERER, cunningly biding his or her time, chooses a victim, and strikes. There is a scream: the victim falls. After the scream, no one except the MURDERER may move.

The Detective re-enters, throwing on the lights and shouting "Everyone freeze". They may question anyone they choose, but may only ask once the question: "Are you the Murderer?" Everyone except the MURDERER must answer truthfully when questioned. For an average-sized party the DETECTIVE may make one false guess at the Murderer's identity — if he or she fails twice, the case is lost. If confronted, the MURDERER must confess.

THE MINISTER'S CAT

*T*his game is a trifle less intellectually demanding than most of the others depicted in this monogram, and so may appeal particularly to those with a childish disposition. The task is to seek out adjectives that may be applied to the MINISTER'S CAT,[1] with each succeeding circuit of adjectives commencing with the same letter. For instance, the first player may say: "The Minister's Cat is an *angry* cat"; the next may say: "The Minister's Cat is an *arrogant* cat"; and so around the company until all are done. Then a new round may start with a statement of this type: "The Minister's Cat is a *bountiful* cat"; and thus until the letters of the alphabet are done. Since the last person in the circuit has, of course, the most difficult task, it is customary that she be elected to initiate the succeeding round.

[1] Should it be that the Minister has no cat, this game may be played equally well using his dog.

CAKE RACE

REQUIREMENTS: *paper plates, gooey cake*.

Each player has his or her hands tied behind them, or is honour bound not to remove their hands from behind their backs. They are placed on their knees, with a paper plate in front of them bearing a large slice of gooey cake. In the interests of fairness *PORTIONS MUST BE EQUAL*. At the signal, the players may start to eat. The player to win is the first to lick their plate clear and flick it back over their heads **WITH NO FLYING CRUMBS OR GOOEY DISCHARGE**.

TOUCH *and* SMELL

For "touch", ask for *three or four volunteers*, who are then blindfolded and have a peg put on their nose. Bring in a tray on which there are eight to ten dishes holding different objects or substances – such as blancmange; butter; dried beans; ketchup; a tennis ball with an apple; silk stockings or a sock; a tea bag; a bar of soap with a lump of cheese; thick canned vegetable soup; a dollop of peanut butter, and other things that I am sure will come to mind. The volunteers must guess what they are feeling – the highest score wins.

For "smell", much the same routine takes place, except the peg is removed from the nose! The volunteers must not be allowed to touch the objects, only to sniff as they are held up to them. Good substances are talcum powder; cheese; olive oil; lemons; wine or brandy; cocoa powder; canned tomatoes; old raw eggs; vanilla essence; potato peelings; old apples; socks, and so on.

THE REVEREND WHITAKER'S ALTERNATIVE

The game of *CONSEQUENCE* is omitted from this book; not purely because it is already well known in every household, but also because it can easily descend into the kind of earthiness that may be acceptable among the manual classes, but certainly has no place in the Drawing-room. However, the Rev. Dr. S. Murray Whitaker of Harlesden has sent to me this alternative version, which may be used to good *educational benefit*, and which will doubtless elicit a moral that all may contemplate as afterwards they retire to their sleeping apartments.

Each player must be equipped with *eight sheets of paper and a pencil*. First, all must determine the type of narrative that is to be created: whether it be a tale of romance and adventure; a mystery yarn; a tale of

virtue derived from a worthy text; or whichever. (All types of stories may be moulded, by the Good Lord's will, until they become tales of virtue; so let the most frivolous among you have his way in this selection. We will imagine that the company has determined upon an *adventurous romance*.) Names are chosen for HERO, HEROINE and VILLAIN. When the "START" is given, the players must write a paragraph or so, describing the background of the tale and the setting into which they wish first to place their HERO. When all are done, they put their topmost sheet now to the bottom of their pile; and pass that pile to the player at their left hand; whereupon all ready themselves for the next page of the narrative.

The nature of the text in each page must be strictly controlled; the pages are ordered thus:

1. The background and setting.
2. A description of the HERO; **his manfulness;** his probity; his predisposition towards virtue . . .

      3. His purpose in undertaking a quest; his destination and what he aspires to find there; his high-minded motives . . .
      4. His enthralling journey through hostile regions;

his battles with monstrous beings; the opportunities he grasps to perform small charities . . .

5. His discovery of the damsel in distress; her beauty and virtue; his admiration for her purity . . .

6. His bold exploits rescuing her from the base clutches of the VILLAIN; the hideousness of the VILLAIN; his bestial practices contrasted with the lofty ethics of the HERO; at last the maid is released and the VILLAIN thwarted!

7. The triumphal return of the HERO and HEROINE, and their betrothal to the gratification of the HERO'S FATHER and MOTHER . . .

8. **A MORAL CONCLUSION**

Of all of these, item no **8.** is of course the most important; and the players may regard it as of sufficient gravity that they defer its completion until the remainder of the tales are read as a whole. For indeed the tales must now be read aloud; and long and loud may be the gales of mirth evinced by their serendipitous juxtapositions, not of like with like, but, more often than not, of *like* with *unlike!* After this, the most senior and (one would expect) most revered of the company may be requested to supply morals for all the tales, drawing upon his own well of knowledge and piety; and thus will he ensure, as we noted above, that each and every story, no matter its nature, may be used to cast light, rather than obscure it.

MERCHANTS

This is a *light-hearted game* for any number of players; but perhaps four or five is the best number. To begin with, one of the company is selected to be a *"MERCHANT"*, and it is then his task to determine which particular sort of wares he will *"sell"* to the others. His fancy may settle upon eggs, or flour, or bread, or any other sensible commodity; we shall assume for our description that he has fixed upon eggs. In order to *"clinch a sale"*, as we may boldly describe his success, he must persuade each of his potential *"customers"* in turn to employ either the name of the commodity or the words *"Yes"*, *"No"*, or *"I"*, in their responses to him; while it is conversely, of course, his rivals' part to do their utmost to avoid using those expressions, while yet responding quite correctly to his harassments.

The conversation might therefore run like this:

"Do you want some eggs today?"

"None are needed, thank you."

"*Then won't you be wanting some for tomorrow?*"

"My family has not the need of any."

"*None at all?*"

"Nary a one, o importunate sir. Now, be off with . . ."

"*But then what will you have for your breakfast?*"

"Devilled kidneys."

"*No eggs with your kidneys?*"

"No . . ."

It is harder than it might seem to avoid permitting the *"MERCHANT"* his *"sale"* in a dialogue such as this; often no more than one or two exchanges are required. Having gained his first *"customer"*, the *"MERCHANT"* must now pass on to the next possible *"client"*; and so forth until he has had his way with all of them; at which point, it is time for the next competitor to take his turn. The winner is the *"MERCHANT"* who is generally adjudged to have prevailed over all his *"customers"* in the shortest overall period of time.

KISS *and* TELL

◆

*Arrange all the ladies present in a circle
around one of the men: this "victim" should be
one of the less shrewd of your friends, and it
helps if he considers himself a "LADIES' MAN"
(regardless of what the ladies think of him!)
Tell him that he will have the chance of being
kissed by whoever he ends up facing, and, having allowed him to memorize the order in which
the ladies are arranged, blindfold him, and
spin him around three times. He is then allowed
to revolve himself until he believes he is facing*

the lady of his choice. When he comes to a standstill, all present should let out a suggestive cheer, as though he has lighted, indeed, on the extremely pretty girl on whom he has had his eye. Meanwhile, one of the gentlemen present — necessarily well-shaven — should silently step into the circle to make the promised kiss. [Kissing on the lips is not advised for this game, as it is unhealthy, and can cause offense: earnibbling has been found to be quite erotic enough, whilst sufficiently impersonal to allow the protagonists to shake hands later without regret.] The kisser then retires quietly from the circle, and the victim is told to take off the blindfold and see which girl kissed him. The group must decide for itself at what stage to reveal the name of the real kisser . . .

THE ELEMENTS

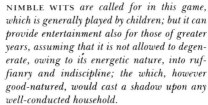

NIMBLE WITS *are called for in this game, which is generally played by children; but it can provide entertainment also for those of greater years, assuming that it is not allowed to degenerate, owing to its energetic nature, into ruffianry and indiscipline; the which, however good-natured, would cast a shadow upon any well-conducted household.*

First a handkerchief or scarf must be tied into a loose knot, so that it may be thrown surely through the air; but yet will be light enough not to cause damage, whatsoever it might hit. This handkerchief is thrown from each to each among the players; before a player throws, he must cry the name of one of the three elements **"EARTH"**, **"AIR"**, *or* **"WATER"**. *On the act of throwing he must start counting rapidly up to*

*ten. The person to whom the missile is thrown must not only catch it, but immediately on so doing, call out the name of a creature that dwells in the apposite element; and certainly the name must be given before the thrower has reached the count of ten. Thus, if the element named is "*WATER*", the catcher may say: "*OCTOPUS*", or "*WHALE*", or "*CRAB*", or "*SALMON*"; if "*AIR*", then any bird or flying insect; and likewise, if "*EARTH*", any beast that dwells on or in the ground, such as "*ELE-PHANT*", or "*EARTHWORM*". In the confusion of catching, and under the urgings of time, this may not be easy to do; contrariwise, while the mind is puzzling to recall a name, it is no simple trick to catch the missile, especially if, as so often happens, it is carelessly and inaccurately cast.*

THE ENDLESS STORY

If the speculations of the anthropologists are to be believed, then our distant ancestors, in the times after the *Fall*, devised the very first of all tales while sitting around their troglodytic fires and passing the telling of some far-fetched yarn between them, one to one, until the tale was done to the satisfaction of all; and then it was remembered by them all and passed on by their lips to others, who had not been there when the tapestry was woven, and who regarded it as being reality, not phantasy. Such imaginings about our ancestors are, of course, for all that our anthropologists deem themselves wiser men than I, tenuous in the extreme – one may scour the Pentateuch

in vain seeking any such description – yet they are reflected prettily in this chaste parlour game.

One of the company volunteers to serve as **MASTER TIME-KEEPER**: he must be set aside a little from the others, with a piece in front of him; and a bell that he may ring. At the first tiny peal of this bell, the first of the players begins a story. There are no restrictions as to the subject or nature of his fabulation, but it is to be hoped that he will take advantage of the opportunity to uplift the company with the tone of his discourse. At the conclusion of precisely *one minute*, **MASTER TIME-KEEPER** rings the bell once more, and the introductory speaker must discontinue his narration. The baton of the tale is passed to the next member of the gathering, who must take it up exactly where it was left off, even should that have been at the midpoint of a sentence. His continuation of the tale must be consistent with what has gone before; yet that need not preclude him from introducing new characters and incidents, very much as MR. CHAS. DICKENS was, *in my estimate*, over-prone to do. Even so, at the end of exactly *one minute*, then, once again, **MASTER TIME-KEEPER** his bell doth toll; and now it is the turn of the next spinner of legends to carry on.

So the game proceeds until all have had their say; then, once more, it is the shift of he who first incepted the tale to accord it its conclusion. This he must do taking into account the *whole* that has gone before; all the digressions and caprices of those that have preceded him must be taken into the reckoning; so that his task is a far from easy one: especially in that he has only *one minute* in which to accomplish all!

Should he fail to conclude the story in a manner satisfactory to all, most notably **MASTER TIME-KEEPER**, he must pay a *forfeit*; otherwise, he may count himself satisfied by the accolade of his fellows. Whichever the event, the burden now passes to the next player to the original's left, to instigate a fresh story.

SHADOW BUFF

S ome *fair degree* of preparation is required for the playing of this excellent diversion; so it is as wise to reserve it only for some festive gathering, when the company will be already great, and the servants busy enough with other duties that one extra will make no difference.

The largest sheet in the house must be pressed into service, and pinned either across the width of the room, or at the least across its corner, so that there is a goodly space left on either side of it. In the smaller of the areas thus defined, place a *chair*, upon which each competitor will seat themselves in their turn; on the other side position a brilliant *lantern* – maybe two or more might be better advised – such that the face of the sheet is brightly illumined. When the time for the game to commence arrives, the first of the players must retire behind the sheet. Now it is the part of the remainder to

traverse the room, one after the other, such that their shadow is cast upon the sheet; it falls to MASTER SINGLETON to cry out his guesses as to the possessor of each *silhouette*. To baffle and bamboozle MASTER SINGLETON, the merry-makers may disguise their outlines using cushions or other similar artifice; or they may slouch as they walk, to camouflage their height; or use whatever other devices their ingenuities may conjure forth.

MASTER SINGLETON should not be informed when he has made a correct guess; but when all the company have performed as required, the total number of MASTER SINGLETON's correct guesses should be totted; and then it is another's turn to retreat into solitude behind the sheet. Once each has had his turn, the scores are reckoned; and he who has supposed most successfully is adjudged triumphant.

THE MISSING GOLDFISH

or a dinner party, set as a table centre a bowl with a single *very small goldfish*. Much comment should be made about the new pet before the meal commences. With everyone in on the joke except one **victim**, who is seated closest to the fishbowl, announce that the first of the evening's games is to eat the soup course blindfolded. Everyone except the victim removes their blindfolds as soon as the dishes are passed around. While the soup – which should, ideally, be a nice crunchy *Gazpacho* – is being eaten a small piece of bread should be dropped into the victim's bowl, making a soft splash. If he or she remarks on this, all should deny hearing anything. At the same time the goldfish should be quietly taken out of the bowl (and placed safely in another bowl next door). All then re-tie their blindfolds, and, as the course is finished, remove them, together with the victim, while generally remarking what a lame and pathetic game it had been. No comment should be made on the missing goldfish until the victim spots it has gone. The hostess should then *feign hysteria*, telling how the poor little thing had jumped out of its bowl on several previous occasions. The party should commence to search the room . . .

DETECTIVE

◆

One player is sent out of the room; he is to be the *THIEF*. The rest stand in a large circle, facing inwards, and with fairly large gaps between. They choose one of themselves as the *plain-clothes man,* or detective. Then they throw a handkerchief on to the middle of the floor, and loudly call in the *THIEF*.

He comes in and enters the ring. His object is to snatch up the handkerchief and escape with it. What makes his job rather nerve-racking is that he does not know which of those standing round is the **DETECTIVE**, and so cannot anticipate from which direction he will be soundly pounced upon as soon as he touches the handkerchief.

Providing the *THIEF* gets safely out of the ring, with the handkerchief, he is allowed to take the place of the **DETECTIVE**, who in turn goes out of the room. But if the *THIEF* is caught before he clears the ring then he must go out again, and a fresh **DETECTIVE** will then be chosen.

No other player in the ring but the **DETECTIVE** is allowed to move – there must be no closing of gaps or obstructing to prevent his escape.

FEEDING *the* ZOO

~

Get all your people seated cross-legged in a ring, giving them no inkling of the trick you propose to play on them. Put down on the floor, in the middle of the circle, a bun or biscuit, or anything edible and appetizing (a chocolate cake has been found to be most tempting of all). Say that you are going to give each person secretly the name of some animal, which none may divulge to another. Then go around and whisper to all the same word – **"ELEPHANT"**.

You now explain that when any player hears this name called they must at once rush forward and seize the food. Begin to call out names very slowly – *Bear . . . Lion . . . Deer . . . Giraffe.* Pause occasionally, as though perplexed, and remind the players to keep their own animal name in mind. Then . . . *Monkey . . . Turtle . . . Dog . . .* and finally . . . ***Elephant!!***

The next moment there will be a confused pile of bodies over the cake.

BUTTON *and* FUNNEL

*C*hoose two gullible male guests. Into the trouser waist of each place a funnel, and give each a button. Tell them that on the signal they must balance their button on their forehead, and then drop it down into the funnel. The first to do so will win a prize. Shout "Go!".

Meanwhile, two ladies present have been given pints of water. As the two contestants look up to position their buttons, the ladies step forward and pour the water into the funnels.

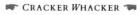

CRACKER WHACKER

*E*ach person present has *six cream crackers* or water biscuits tied to their head with a ribbon, and is given a bathroom loufa (if you don't have half a dozen or so to hand, rolled newspapers are an acceptable substitute). At the cry of **"CRACKER WHACKER"** there is a free-for-all, and everyone can lay about them. The last contestant with a cracker intact is the winner. *Warning:* The Publishers strongly recommend the wearing of swimming goggles when playing this game.

THERE'LL BE THE D...L TO PAY.

WAITER *and* WAITRESS STUNTS

---◆---

If you are holding an event at a restaurant, visit beforehand to set up one of the following *amusing* stunts:

THE POMPOUS WAITER

*Let all of your friends except the victim know that the game is afoot. When the waiter arrives to take the orders, everything will go smoothly until the victim orders his or her meal, when the waiter, briefed (and possibly bribed) beforehand, will start to argue, and show disdain for the **victim's choice of food**. "Surely not the liver followed by chocolate fudge. Well, if you are sure . . ." and so on. When the waiter leaves, the victim will look to the party for support and sympathy, but the party should be non-committal: "Actually, I think he had a point, it was a rather odd choice," etc. When the waiter comes back to take the order for wine, the victim should be nominated by all to take the list. Then things get really lively, as the waiter refuses outright to take the order: "I'm afraid that really won't do – you obviously know nothing about wine. You must be aware of the sort of establishment this is – this is really most embarrassing". The other guests at this point look deeply ashamed of their friend . . .*

THE JUMPING WAITRESS

*A man, in this instance, should be the victim —
NO-ONE ELSE should be in on the joke. Every
time the waitress comes by, to bring bread,
water, take orders, and so on, she should position herself by the man in question, and
periodically give a little leap, so that everyone
notices, and it becomes a subject of remark
between courses. At some point in the evening
the waitress should make a show of standing
prominently in the restaurant, talking to the
manager in an animated fashion. As the last
course is being served, the waitress should pro-
claim loudly — drawing the attention to all in*

the restaurant – *"I'm sorry, Sir, but this is the final straw. You have touched me* EVERY TIME *I have been to this table"* (and so on). *At this stage the manager should arrive at the table and put his arm around the girl to comfort her, while glaring at the victim. Choose for yourself when to reveal the nature of the stunt: I know of one extreme instance where the caper was taken one step further, when the manager feigned to* **call the police**, *and two uniformed actors arrived to caution and "arrest" the individual in question!*

FORFEITS: A NOTE

In all the games that we ladies and gentlemen play among each other – yes, and children, too – there must inevitably come a time when some are declared the **VICTOR** and others the **LOSER**; this latter designation may reduce the Youngest Ones among us to tears, but we should not therefore take mercy upon them; for the small reverses of youth serve their purpose, in building up the moral fibre of the adult who is yet dormant within the child. It is, however, not unreasonable to give each child a trivial sweetmeat of some kind at the game's conclusion, to reinforce our adage that it is the taking-part, and not the **triumph**, that is important. Com-

plementarily, one must severely chastise any child, no matter how youthful he might be, who sees fit to revel in his glory, taunting his fellows with it.

Among adults, save those of a dastardly dicing disposition, it is customary for small FORFEITS *to be exacted from those who have in some wise defaulted or erred during the playing of a game; or who have perhaps simply come last of all; where the shame of their failure in the race is insufficient to register their misdoing. In some households it is the practice that miscreants should forfeit articles from among their possessions – such as buttons and bangles – but among the God-fearing such customs are rightly frowned upon; for may they not be thought of as **vile GAMBLING**, sneaking, cunningly disguised as by the **Devil Himself**, into the bosom of one's family? At the very least, they are the wedge's less broad end. And so have come about the charming **Forfeits** that those in more virtuous and Godly homes may exact upon their fellows. More comprehensive lists of these winsome rituals may be found in greater books than this; the following is but a selection; and nor are there any of the **libidinous** and unseemly forfeits given, as the Rev. Joh. Clute (a Methodist, but even so!) has brazenly elected to include in his obscene and bestial work; I refer of course to those in which kisses must promiscuously be exchanged.* 🖛

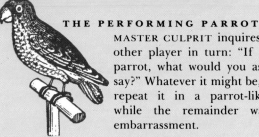

THE PERFORMING PARROT

MASTER CULPRIT inquires of each other player in turn: "If I were a parrot, what would you ask me to say?" Whatever it might be, he must repeat it in a parrot-like voice; while the remainder watch his embarrassment.

THE THREE QUESTIONS

The defaulter is told that he will be asked three questions, to which he must respond with only either a "YEA", or a "NAY". These answers he must give now, before the questions are in fact posed. Picture the confusion caused to his sensibilities once the others have formulated their questions!

TONGUE TWISTERS

MASTER CULPRIT must recite a torturously phrased sentence or verse to the satisfaction of his companions; until he succeeds the forfeit is not deemed to have been paid. Here is an exemplar for the sake of those incapable of devising one for themselves:

> *Being in the garden I saw three brave maids, by three broad beds, braiding broad braids. I said: "Bravo", bravely to the three brave maids, braiding broad braids beside broad beds; "Braid broad braids, brave maids."*

CHOOSING AN ACTION

One of the spectators makes three gestures behind the back of MASTER CULPRIT, who must not see those gestures. Then the miscreant is required to select one of the three, by number. They might perhaps be a shake of the hand, a bending of the knee, and a boxing of the ears. Whichever compliment MASTER CULPRIT selects, that shall be paid to him.

PUT TWO CHAIRS TOGETHER,
TAKE OFF YOUR SHOES,
AND JUMP OVER 'EM

This is an easy forfeit for those with their wits about them, for of course it is the shoes that are jumped over!

THE LIVING STATUE

MASTER CULPRIT is told to remove his shoes and to stand upon a chair. Poised there, he must adopt whatever pose the company command; and hold it until such time as they deem the forfeit well paid. 🖙

RAPID CHANGES

The unfortunate MASTER CULPRIT must take his left ear with his right hand, and his nose with his left hand. Then he is told to exchange the positions of his hands, and again, and again; the rapidity of the repetition being accelerated until such time as he is rendered helpless. Some victims cause great hilarity by performing with such zeal that they smite themselves!

FRIEND

MASTER CULPRIT must go to each of the other participants in turn and bestow upon them a companionable smile. In practice, this forfeit can be more difficult than it might seem!

SLIPPERY HOG

*T*o break the ice at any gathering, it is a fine idea to keep to hand a small pig called *Gertie*. The little hog should be liberally greased and kept conveniently in the next room. Tell your guests that you are expecting another visitor – *Gertie* – who is a real sport, and that there will be a prize for the first person who can catch and hold her for ten seconds. Having excited them to a state of frenzy, open the door, let in your tiny porcine pal, then stand back and watch the fun!

FINIS